TOP COUNTRY SONGS OF THE 70'S

Billboard®

Photographs courtesy of The Country Music Foundation, Inc.

ISBN 0-7935-0947-5

Billboard is a trademark of BPI Communications
Used by permission.
The chart and popularity data used herein is reproduced by permission of BPI Communications.
Copyright 1970-1979 BPI Communications.

HL® Hal Leonard Publishing Corporation

7777 West Bluemound Road P.O. Box 13819 Milwaukee, WI 53213

Billboard. TOP COUNTR

SONGS OF THE 70's

As a time when major careers were being launched and important musical trends established, the 1970s were a particularly rich decade. These were the years that gave us the CB (citizen's band) radio craze and the very brief period in which America's pop stars became country music's top stars. But the most significant musical event of the era, without a doubt, was the 1976 release on RCA Records of an album called, *Wanted! The Outlaws*. It contained previously issued songs by Waylon Jennings, Willie Nelson, Tompall Glaser and Jessi Colter. Not only did it become the first million-selling country album, it ushered in the hip, cowboy-flavored music that has survived into the '90s.

Introduction

By Edward Morris

Furthermore, that album went a long way toward elevating Jennings and Nelson from interesting performers to superstars. Although Jennings and Nelson had been appearing on the country charts since the 1960s, Jennings did not have a No. 1 hit until 1974, when he scored with "This Time." Nelson had to wait a year longer to see his "Blue Eyes Cryin' In The Rain" go to the top. Neither Glaser nor Colter (who is Jennings' wife) experienced similar success. However, Colter did enjoy one No. 1 hit, "I'm Not Lisa," in 1975. Had Jennings and Nelson not spread their music to a younger audience, one that was more accustomed to rock music than country, it is doubtful that the *Urban Cowboy* craze of the early '80s would have ever occurred. It is only a slight oversimplification to say that none of the major country acts was wearing cowboy hats in 1970 but nearly all of them were by 1980. Once established, "Waylon & Willie" ruled the charts and the concert halls with such hits as "A Good Hearted Woman" (1976) and "Mammas Don't Let Your Babies Grow Up To Be Cowboys" (1978).

Jessi Colter

Waylon Jennings

Willie Nelson

Tanya Tucker

Eddie Rabbitt

The decade saw the breakthrough and rise of such stars as Tanya Tucker, Eddie Rabbitt, Moe Bandy, John Conlee, T.G. Sheppard, Mickey Gilley, and the Oak Ridge Boys. Tucker was a mere 13 years old when she had her first Top 10 hit, "Delta Dawn," in 1972. Before she turned 14, she scored two No. 1s, "What's Your Mama's Name" and "Blood Red And Going Down." Rabbitt got his start as a songwriter; but he had made his mark as a singer by the mid-70s. By the time his "Every Which Way But Loose" (from the Clint Eastwood movie of the same name) went No. 1 in 1979, Rabbitt could look back at a string of chart-toppers. Moe Bandy was a throw-back to the hard-living, hard-singing honky-tonkers of Hank Williams' day. He first charted in 1974 with "I Just Started Hatin' Cheatin' Songs Today" and carried that theme forward to 1979 with the No. 2 hit, "It's A Cheating Situation."

Oak Ridge Boys

A former disc jockey and undertaker, John Conlee decided during the late '70s that he had what it took to be a country singer. He made his debut with "Rose Colored Glasses" in 1978. His next single, "Lady Lay Down," became his first No. 1 the following year. T. G. Sheppard had promoted records for other singers under his real name, William Browder, when the singing bug bit him. With a new name and a great song — "Devil In The Bottle" — Sheppard went No. 1 in 1974 — his first time out. He had two more No. 1s during the decade, the final one being "The Last Cheater's Waltz." Mickey Gilley, who sang and played piano a lot like his cousin, Jerry Lee Lewis, had a minor hit in 1968 on a small Louisiana label. But he went straight to the top in 1974 with "Room Full Of Roses." He would become outrageously famous six years later when the Texas nightclub that bore his name became the site and focal point of the movie, *Urban Cowboy*. The Oak Ridge Boys started out in the 1940s as the Oak Ridge Quartet, a gospel group. And the group stayed gospel until it was lured to country music in the early 1970s. After a slow start, the Oaks found their entry into the big-time in 1977 with "Y'All Come Back Saloon." It went to No. 3 as did another of their most requested songs, "Come On In," which charted in 1979.

Another bright new voice of the period was Ronnie Milsap. Classically trained, Milsap nonetheless found himself veering toward rhythm & blues and country music when it came time to start his career. He made a bow into country in 1973 with the fiercely titled "I Hate You." His first No. 1 was "Pure Love" (1974), an Eddie Rabbitt composition. Milsap showed his range and popularity by scoring No. 1s with songs as different as the hard-country "Daydreams About Night Things" to the sweetly pop "It Was Almost Like A Song."

In the mid-1970s, the country music industry went out of its way to show it was open to outside influences. In spite of protest from older country acts, the Country Music Association voted pop singer Olivia Newton-John its female vocalist of the year award in 1974. And in 1975, the CMA gave John Denver its highest accolade, entertainer of the year, and named his hit, "Back Home Again," song of the year. In fact, Denver enjoyed three No. 1 country hits that year, "Back Home Again," "Thank God I'm A Country Boy" and "I'm Sorry." A year earlier, even ex-Beatle Paul McCartney made his way into the country record books with "Sally G." However, it climbed only to No. 51 before tumbling off the charts.

When OPEC temporarily cut off America's oil supply in 1973, it severely raised the price of gasoline and ultimately led to the fuel conservation measure of lowering the speed-limit on America's highways to 55-miles-an-hour. As this was occurring, electronics manufacturers were introducing to the public low-cost CB radios. Not surprisingly, these social upheavals were felt in country music as elsewhere. Truckers — who had long rivaled cowboys as heroes in country song — began using their CB radios to evade speedtraps and over-zealous cops. Soon, the brave and lovable trucker became a country folk-hero, via such chronicles as C. W. McCall's "Convoy" (1975), Cledus Maggard's "The White Knight" (1975), Jerry Reed's "East Bound And Down" (1977), and Red Sovine's classic weeper, "Teddy Bear" (1976). While country's interest in CB radios has died, the romantic trucker figure drives on and, presumably, into tomorrow.

Several of the most memorable songs of the 1970s were sung by performers who — for this reason or that — never seemed able to stay in the front ranks for long. Among those were "Help Me Make It Through The Night" (1971), Sammi Smith's biggest hit and only No. 1; Kenny Starr's "Blind Man In The Bleachers" (1976), his only Top 10; Johnny Russell's "Rednecks, White Socks And Blue Ribbon Beer" (1973), his only Top 10; and Cal Smith's "Country Bumpkin" (1974), the second of a career total of three No. 1s.

Mickey Gilley

Ronnie Milsap

Tom T. Hall

Kenny Rogers

*10-4
Good
Buddy!*

Both creatively and chart-wise, Tom T. Hall was a giant during most of the '70s. He wrote his own songs, almost always emphasizing the narrative, and he sang them as if he were telling a story, not acting it out. He had seven No. 1s and 10 Top 10s between 1970 and 1980. Merle Haggard, Loretta Lynn, George Jones, Charlie Rich, Conway Twitty, and Charley Pride maintained the momentum during the decade that they had gained in the '60s. Jones and Tammy Wynette, who was then his wife, had a series of duet hits in the '70s, including the No. 1 "Golden Ring" (1976).

Pop emigré Kenny Rogers found a home in country in 1977 when "Lucille" made it to the chart-peak. "The Gambler" (1978) was an even bigger hit, giving Rogers a movie story-theme that he still works. Musically, Dolly Parton went in the other direction, abandoning her long-time mentor and partner, Porter Wagoner, in the late '70s to explore pop music, television and the movies.

The old "outlaw," Willie Nelson, co-starred with Robert Redford in *The Electric Horseman* (1979), thereby helping pave the way for the boots of the urban cowboy as the '70s came to an end.

AMANDA

Words and Music by
BOB McDILL

I've held it____ all in - ward,____ Lord knows I've tried.
meas - ure____ of peo - ple____ don't un - der - stand

It's an aw - ful____ awak - 'ning____ in a coun - try boy's____ life.
the pleas - ures____ of life in____ a hill - bil - ly____ band.

To look in____ the mir - ror____ in to - tal sur - prise____
I got my first____ gui - tar____ when I was four - teen,____

fate should have made you a gen - tle - man's wife.

Well, a

wife.

(HEY, WON'T YOU PLAY)
ANOTHER SOMEBODY DONE SOMEBODY WRONG SONG

Words and Music by LARRY BUTLER
and CHIPS MOMAN

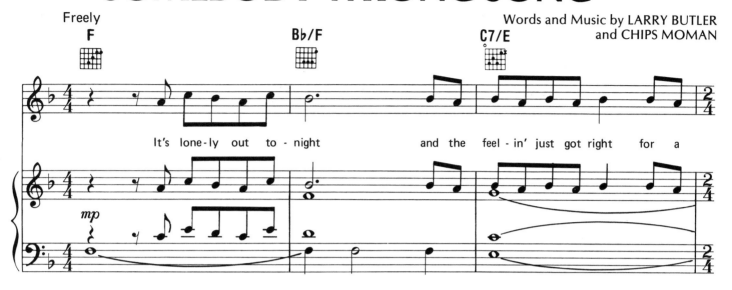

It's lone-ly out to-night and the feel-in' just got right for a

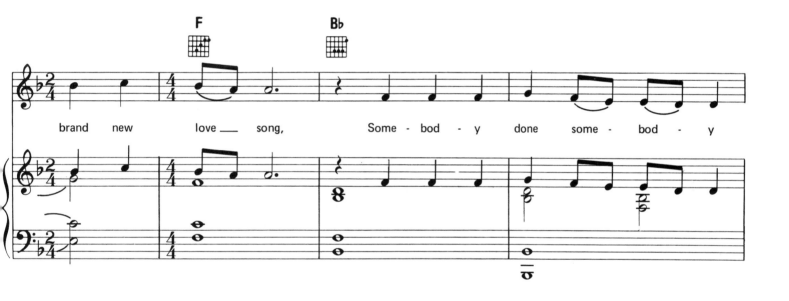

brand new love ___ song, Some-bod-y done some-bod-y

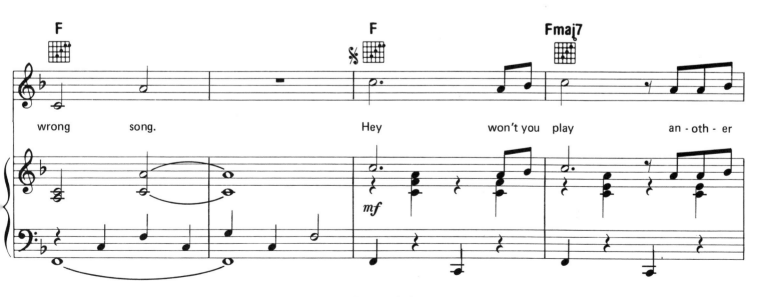

wrong song. Hey won't you play an-oth-er

ARE YOU SURE HANK DONE IT THIS WAY

Words and Music by
WAYLON JENNINGS

Moderate Country

BEST THING THAT EVER HAPPENED TO ME

Words and Music by
JIM WEATHERLY

BLIND MAN IN THE BLEACHERS

Words and Music by
STERLING WHIPPLE

He's just the blind man in the bleach-ers

to the lo - cal home - town fans.

And he sits be-neath the speak-ers way back in the

BURGERS AND FRIES

Words and Music by
BEN PETERS

Burg-ers and fries and cher-ry pies, it was sim-ple and good back then.

Walk-in' in the sand, hand in hand, nev-er think-in' that it could end. Mak-in' our love with the moon a - bove at the

drive - in pic-ture show. It was burg-ers and fries and cher-ry pies in a world we used to know.

Well, I'm Chan - ges come and go still the same ol' me. we've had our share, I know. Now it That's all that I'll ev - er be. I'd

BLOOD RED AND GOING DOWN

Words and Music by
CURLY PUTMAN

Moderately slow

That Geor-gia sun was blood-red and go-ing down,____ that

Geor-gia sun was blood-red and go-ing down.

1. Dad-dy said: "Now come, girl." We head-ed down the road to Au-gus-ta,____
2. With dusty tear-drops on his face my dad-dy cried and big steps he was taking;
3. We search-ed in ev-er-y bar room and hon-ky tonk as well,____

and faint - ly through his clenched teeth, he called ma-ma's name, and then he
half - way run - ning to keep up, my short legs were so tired they were
and fi - nal - ly dad - dy found them, Lord, you know the rest is hard

F7

Bb

cussed her._____
shak - ing._____
to tell._____

He said, "Girl, you're young,__ but some
"Where did I go____wrong, girl,
He sent me out_____to wait,

F

dude has come a-long and stole your moth-er."
and why would she leave us both this way?"
but scared, I look-ed back through the door,

But you can't steal a will-in' mind,__'cause
At times like these a girl of__ten,
and dad - dy left them both soak -

CAROLYN

Words and Music by
TOMMY COLLINS

COME ON IN

By MICHAEL CLARK

COUNTRY BUMPKIN

Words and Music by
DON WAYNE

COUNTRY SUNSHINE

Words and Music by DOTTIE WEST
and BILL DAVIS

I was raised on coun-try sun - shine, green grass be-neath my feet,

run-nin' through fields of dai-sies, wad-in' through the creek. You love me and it's in-

vit-in'___ to go where life is more ex-cit-in', but I was raised __ on coun-try

DAYDREAMS ABOUT NIGHT THINGS

Words and Music by
JOHN SCHWEERS

THE DOOR IS ALWAYS OPEN

Words and Music by BOB McDILL
and DICKEY LEE

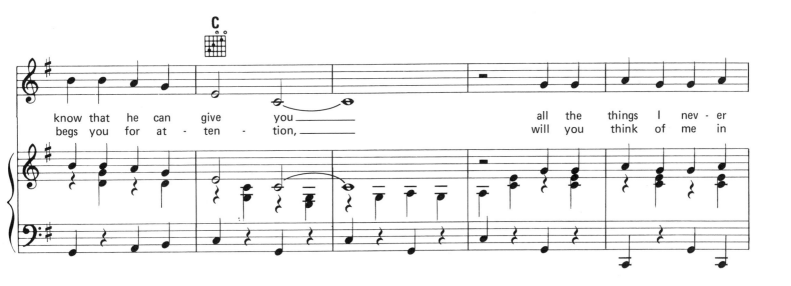

D **G7** **C**

could. _____
stead? _____

But I know that he won't give you _____
And when he reach-es out to touch you, _____

D **G**

_____ what you need ___ most of all. _____
is your face turned to-ward the wall? _____

Csus **C** **D**

Well,
Yes, { the door is al-ways o - pen, _____ and the

D7 **G** **F** **C** **G**

light's on in the hall. Yes, the door ___ is al-ways

o - pen, _____ and the light's _ on in the hall. _____

_____ And you know __ that I'll be wait - in' _____

when you fi - nal - ly come to call.

When night falls on that

EVERY WHICH WAY BUT LOOSE

Words and Music by STEPHEN DORFF,
MILTON BROWN and SNUFF GARRETT

EASY LOVING

Words and Music by FREDDIE HART

THE FIGHTIN' SIDE OF ME

Words and Music by
MERLE HAGGARD

THE GAMBLER

Words and Music by
DON SCHLITZ

we took turns a - star - in' out the win - dow at the dark - ness till
you don't mind my say - in' I can see you're out of ac — es; for a

bore-dom o — ver took us and he be - gan __ to speak. He said
taste of your whis-key I'll

give you some __ ad - vice." 3. So I learn to play __ it right." "You got to

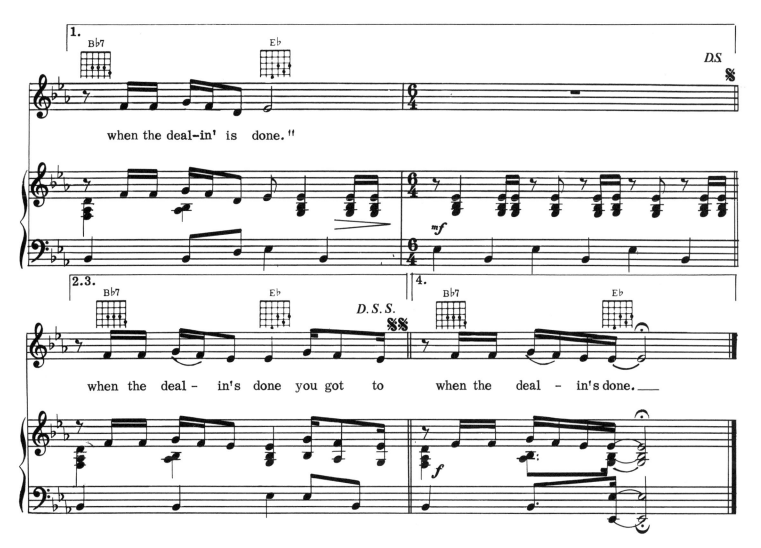

Verse 3:
(So I) handed him my bottle,
And he drank down my last swallow.
Then he bummed a cigarette and
Asked me for a light.
And the night got deathly quiet and
His face lost all expression.
Said, "If you're gonna play the game,
Boy, you gotta (learn to play it right.)"
(To Chorus:)

Verse 4:
"Ev'ry gambler knows that the secret to survivin'
Is knowin' what to throw away, and
Knowin' what to keep.
'Cause ev'ry hand's a winner, and
Ev'ry hand's a loser.
And the best that you can hope for
Is to die in your sleep." And

Verse 5:
When he'd finished speakin'
He turned back toward the window.
Crushed out his cigarette and
Faded off to sleep.
And somewhere in the darkness
The gambler he broke even.
But in his final words I found
An ace that I could keep. (To Chorus:)

A GOOD HEARTED WOMAN

Words and Music by WAYLON JENNINGS
and WILLIE NELSON

GOLDEN RING

Words and Music by BOBBY BRADDOCK
and RAFE VanHOY

HELP ME MAKE IT THROUGH THE NIGHT

Words and Music by
KRIS KRISTOFFERSON

I LOVE

By TOM T. HALL

I MAY NEVER GET TO HEAVEN

Words and Music by BUDDY KILLEN
and BILL ANDERSON

I walked with you and talked with you and held your lov - ing hand.__ We loved a - while; I lived a - while, and thought that fate__ had it planned.

Then some - one stole my an - gel__ and I lost what I loved
once__ I held your sweet love,__ and felt what your ten - der

I AIN'T NEVER

Words and Music by MEL TILLIS
and WEBB PIERCE

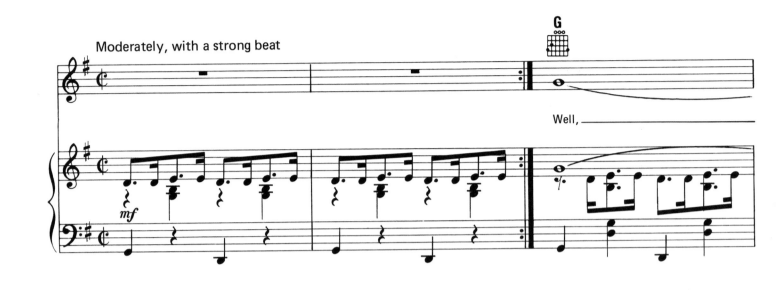

Moderately, with a strong beat

Well, _____

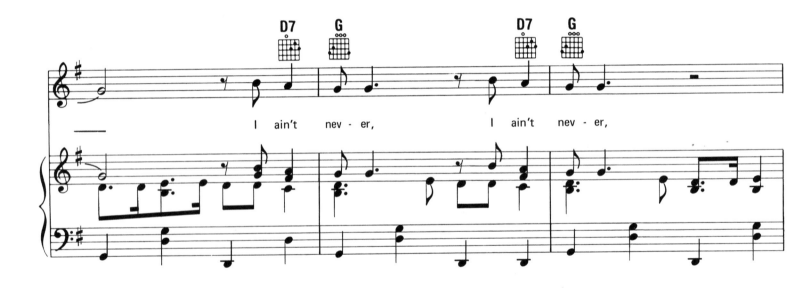

I ain't nev - er, I ain't nev - er,

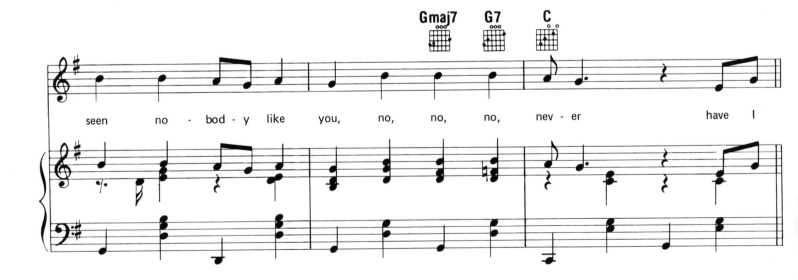

seen no - bod - y like you, no, no, no, nev - er have I

I WOULDN'T WANT TO LIVE
(IF YOU DIDN'T LOVE ME)

Words and Music by
AL TURNEY

Moderate Country 2

Some - times _____ you may think I take you for grant - ed, _____ and
love that makes the world _ go round, and

grant - ed _____ some - times may - be I do, 'cause I've _____
my love for you just grows with leaps _ and bounds, 'cause I've _____

I'M KNEE DEEP IN LOVING YOU

Words and Music by
SONNY THROCKMORTON

I'M NOT LISA

Words and Music by
JESSI COLTER

I'M NOT THROUGH LOVING YOU YET

By CONWAY TWITTY
and L.E. WHITE

Country Waltz (♩ to be played ♪)

You came to me and you threw me with a sim-ple___ good-bye;___ I begged___ your for-give-ness, but you won't___ e-ven try. You just

IF WE MAKE IT THROUGH DECEMBER

Words and Music by
MERLE HAGGARD

IT ONLY HURTS FOR A LITTLE WHILE

Words and Music by MACK DAVID
and FRED SPIELMAN

on - ly hurts for a lit - tle while.__
on - ly hurts for a lit - tle while.__

IS ANYBODY GOIN' TO SAN ANTONE

Words and Music by DAVE KIRBY
and GLENN MARTIN

Moderate Country 2

Rain drip-ping off the brim of my hat,___ sure is cold to-
Wind whip-pin' down the neck of my shirt like I ain't got noth - in'

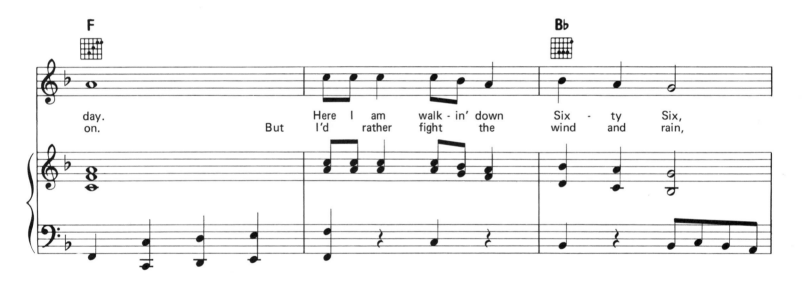

day.
on. But Here I am walk-in' down the Six - ty Six, wind and rain,

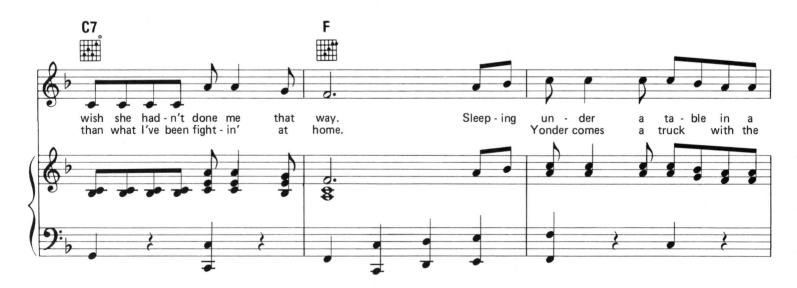

wish she had-n't done me that way. Sleep-ing un-der a ta-ble in a
than what I've been fight - in' at home. Yon-der comes a truck with the

IT WAS ALMOST LIKE A SONG

Lyric by HAL DAVID
Music by ARCHIE JORDAN

Relaxed

Once in ev - 'ry life,
You were in my arms,

some - one comes a -
just where you be -

long,
long,

and you came to me.
we were so in love.

IT'S A CHEATING SITUATION

Words and Music by SONNY THROCKMORNTON
and CURLY PUTMAN

It's a cheat-ing sit-u-a-tion, a steal-ing in-vi-ta-tion, to take what's not real-ly ours to make it through the mid-night hours. It's a cheat-ing sit-u-a-tion, just a cheap im-i-

IT'S ONLY MAKE BELIEVE

Words and Music by CONWAY TWITTY
and JACK NANCE

IT'S NOT LOVE
(BUT IT'S NOT BAD)

Words and Music by GLENN MARTIN
and HANK COCHRAN

LADY LAY DOWN

Words and Music by DON COOK
and RAFE VanHOY

LUCKENBACH, TEXAS
(Back To The Basics Of Love)

Words and Music by BOBBY EMMONS
and CHIPS MOMAN

THE LAST CHEATER'S WALTZ

Words and Music by
SONNY THROCKMORNTON

Moderate Country Waltz

She was

go - ing ___ to piec - es ___ when he walked in the door; She
tells her ___ he loves her ___ and the mu - sic plays on; He

just had ___ to see him ___ she can't wait no more. To - night he'll be
tells her ___ he needs her ___ but some - one's at home. The ball game's all

MISSISSIPPI COTTON PICKIN' DELTA TOWN

Words and Music by HAROLD DORMAN
and WILEY GANN

Medium Fast Country

In a Mis-sis-sip-pi cot-ton pick-ing del-ta town,—

one dust-y street___ to walk up and down.___ (1,2.)Noth-in' much to see but a
(3.)Noth-in' much to do but just

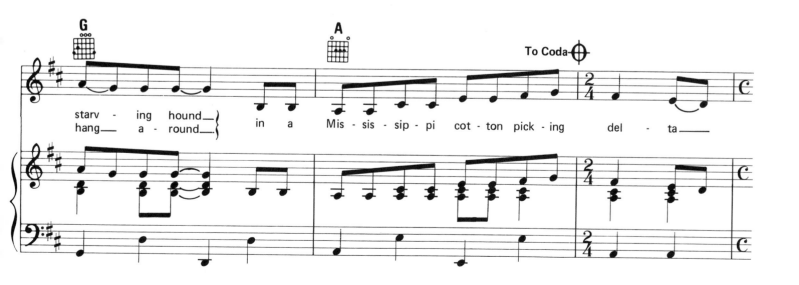

starv-ing hound }
hang___ a-round } in a Mis-sis-sip-pi cot-ton pick-ing del-ta___

To Coda ⊕

MAMMAS DON'T LET YOUR BABIES GROW UP TO BE COWBOYS

Words and Music by ED BRUCE
and PATSY BRUCE

MY ELUSIVE DREAMS

Words and Music by CURLY PUTMAN
and BILLY SHERRILL

2. You had my child in Memphis, I heard of work in Nashville,
   We didn't find it there so we moved on.
   To a small farm in Nebraska to a gold mine in Alaska,
   We didn't find it there so we moved on. (Chorus)

3. And now we've left Alaska because there was no gold mine,
   But this time only two of us move on.
   Now all we have is each other and a little memory to cling to,
   And still you won't let me go on alone. (Chorus)

MISTER LOVE MAKER

Words and Music by
JOHNNY PAYCHECK

OLD DOGS, CHILDREN AND WATERMELON WINE

By TOM T. HALL

Moderato

3. Ever had a drink of watermelon wine? He asked.
   He told me all about it though I didn't answer back.
   Ain't but three things in this world that's worth a solitary dime,
   But OLD DOGS-CHILDREN AND WATERMELON WINE.

4. He said women think about theyselves when menfolk ain't around,
   And friends are hard to find when they discover that you down.
   He said I tried it all when I was young and in my natural prime;
   Now it's OLD DOGS-CHILDREN AND WATERMELON WINE.

5. Old dogs care about you even when you make mistakes.
   God bless little children while they're still too young to hate.
   When he moved away, I found my pen and copied down that line
   'Bout old dogs and children and watermelon wine.

6. I had to catch a plane up to Atlanta that next day,
   As I left for my room I saw him pickin' up my change.
   That night I dreamed in peaceful sleep of shady summertime
   Of old dogs and children and watermelon wine.

ONE PIECE AT A TIME

Words and Music by
WAYNE KEMP

Talking blues tempo

1. Well I left Ken-tuck-y back in for-ty nine and went to De-troit work-in' on as-sem-bly lines. The first year, they had me put-tin' wheels on Cad-il-lacs. Ev-'ry

ride a - round _ in style; I'm gon-na drive ev-'ry-bod - y wild. 'Cause I'll

have the on - ly one there is a - round.

RECITATION

3. So, the very next day when I punched in with my big lunch box
   And with help from my friends, I left that day with a lunch box full of gears.
   I've never considered myself a thief, but GM wouldn't miss just one little piece
   Especially if I strung it out over several years.

4. The first day, I got me a fuel pump, and the next day I got me an engine and a trunk.
   Then, I got me a transmission and all the chrome.
   The little things I could get in the big lunch box
   Like nuts and bolts and all four shocks.
   But the big stuff we snuck out in my buddy's mobile home.

5. Now, up to now, my plan went all right, 'til we tried to put it all together one night.
   And that's when we noticed that something was definitely wrong.
   The transmission was a '53, and the motor turned out to be a '73,
   And when we tried to put in the bolts, all the holes were gone.
   So, we drilled it out so that it would fit, and with a little bit of help from an adapter kit,
   We had the engine running just like a song.

6. Now the headlights, they was another sight,
   We had two on the left, and one on the right.
   But when we pulled out the switch, all three of 'em come on.
   The back end looked kinda funny, too.
   But we put it together, and when we got through, well, that's when we noticed that we only had one tail fin.
   About that time, my wife walked out, and I could see in her eyes that she had her doubts.
   But she opened the door and said, "Honey, take me for a spin."

7. So, we drove uptown just to get the tags, and I headed her right on down the main drag.
   I could hear everybody laughin' for blocks around.
   But, up there at the court house, they didn't laugh,
   'Cause to type it up, it took the whole staff.
   And when they got through, the title weighed sixty pounds.

2nd CHORUS: I got it One Piece At A Time, and it didn't cost me a dime.
              You'll know it's me when I come through your town.
              I'm gonna ride around in style; I'm gonna drive everybody wild,
              'Cause I'll have the only one there is around.

(Ad Lib): "Yeah, Red Rider, this is the Cottonmouth in the Psychobilly Cadillac, com'on? This
              is the Cotton-mouth, a negatory on the cost of this mo-chine, there, Red Rider, you might
              say I went right up to the factory and picked it up, it's cheaper that way. What model is
              it?. . . . .Well, it's a 49, 50, 51, 52, 53, 54, 55, 56. 57. 58. 59 automobile. 60, 61,
              62, 63, 64, 65, 66, 67, 68, 69 automobile. . . . .70, 71, 72, 73. . . . .

REDNECKS, WHITE SOCKS AND BLUE RIBBON BEER

Words and Music by BOB McDILL,
WAYLAND HOLYFIELD and CHUCK NEESE

Lively, with humor

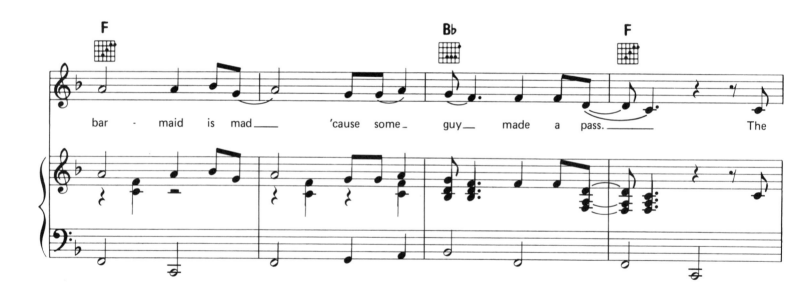

THE ROOTS OF MY RAISING

Words and Music by
TOMMY COLLINS

tri-bute to a way of life that's al-most past and gone.

Chorus:

The roots of my rais - ing run deep. ____

____ I've come back for the strength that I need; ____

____ and hope comes no mat - ter how far down I

sink, 'Cause the roots of my rais - ing run deep.

To Coda ⊕

Recitation:

— I pulled into the driveway, It sure was good to be there.

Then I could see thru the open door that dad was asleep in his favorite chair.

In his hand was a picture of mom, *I remembered how close they*

So I just turned away; I didn't want to wake him and spoil his dream of her.

2. A Christian mom who had the strength for life the way she did,
Then to pull that apron off and do the Charleston for us kids.
Dad, a quiet man who's gentle voice was seldom heard,
Could borrow money at the bank simply on his word.
(Repeat Chorus)

ROOM FULL OF ROSES

Words and Music by
TIM SPENCER

Moderato, with expression

Chorus

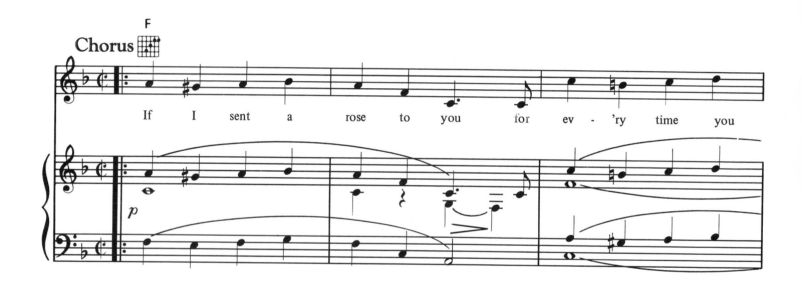

If I sent a rose to you for ev-'ry time you

made me blue, You'd have a Room Full Of Ros - es,

SAWMILL

Words and Music by MEL TILLIS
and HORACE WHATLEY

SHE BELIEVES IN ME

Words and Music by
STEVE GIBB

SHE'S GOT YOU

Words and Music by
HANK COCHRAN

SLEEPING SINGLE IN A DOUBLE BED

Words and Music by DENNIS MORGAN
and KYE FLEMING

Moderately

Sleep-in' sin-gle in a dou-ble bed, ___ think-in' o-ver things I wish I'd ___ said. ___

I should-'ve held you, but I let you go; ___ now I'm the one sleep-in' all a-lone. ___

___ Sleep-in' sin-gle in a dou-ble bed. ___ Toss-in', turn-in', try-in' to for-get. ___

CODA

sin-gle in a dou-ble bed. *Instrumental*

D. S. al Codetta

Codetta

Repeat
and Fade

SHE'S PULLING ME BACK AGAIN

Words and Music by JERRY FOSTER
and BILL RICE

TEDDY BEAR

Words and Music by DALE ROYAL,
BILLY JOE BURNETTE, JOE SOVINE
and TOMMY HILL

Moderately Bright

(Recitation:) I was on the outskirts of a little southern town; trying to reach
my destination before the sun went down......The CB was blaring away on
channel 19...when there came a little boy's voice on the radio line......
He said: "Breaker 19!...Is anyone there? Come on back, truckers...and
talk to Teddy Bear!"......I keyed the mike and said: "You got it, Teddy Bear!"
And a little boy's voice came back on the air......"Preciate the break,......
Who we got on that end?"......
I told him my handle and he began:......

"I'm not supposed to bother you fellows out there......Mom says you're busy and
for me to stay off the air......But you see, I get lonely and it helps to talk...
'cause that's all I can do....I'm crippled,.....I can't walk!!!"

I came back and told him to fire up that mike......and I'd talk to him as long
as he liked......"This was my dad's radio" the little boy said.....'"But I
guess it's mine and mom's now, 'cause my dad's dead!"

"He had a wreck about a month ago..He was trying to get home in a blinding
snow....Mom has to work now, to make ends meet...and I'm not much help with
my two crippled feet!"

"She says not to worry...that we'll make it alright...But I hear her crying
sometimes late at night......There's just one thing I want more than anything to
see......Aw, I know you guys are too busy to bother with me!"

"But my dad used to take me for rides when he was home...but that's all over
now, since my daddy's gone..."...Not one breaker came on the old CB
as the little crippled boy talked with me..I tried to swallow a lump that
wouldn't stay down......as I thought about my boy back in Greenville Town.

"Dad was going to take mom and me with him later on this year....I remember
him saying: 'Someday this old truck will be yours, Teddy Bear!'......But I know
now I will never get to ride an 18 wheeler again......but this old bus will keep
me in touch with all my trucker friends!"

"Teddy Bear's gonna back on out now and leave you alone 'cause it's about time
for mom to come home......Give me a shout when you're passing through......and
I'll surely be happy to come back to you!"

I came back and said: "Before you go, 10 - 10......what's you home 20, little
CB friend?"......He gave me his address and I didn't once hesitate....this
hot load of freight would just have to wait!

I turned that truck around on a dime and headed for Jackson Street, 229.....
I round the corner and got one heck of a shock......18 wheelers were lined up
for three city blocks!

Every driver for miles around had caught Teddy Bear's call....and that little
crippled boy was having a ball......For as fast as one driver would carry him
in, another would carry him to his truck and take off again.

Well, you better believe I took my turn riding Teddy Bear....and then carried
him back in and put him down on his chair....And if I never live to see happiness
again.....I saw it that day in the face of that little man.

We took up a collection for him before his mama got home.....Each driver said
goodbye and then they were gone....He shook my hand with his mile-long grin
and said: "So long, trucker....I'll catch you again!"

I hit the Interstate with tears in my eyes....I turned on the radio and got
another surprise...."Breaker 19!" Came the voice on the air...."Just one word
of thanks from Mama Teddy Bear!"

"We wish each and every one a special prayer for you....you made a little crippled
boy's dream come true.....I'll sign off now, before I start to cry.......
May God ride with you......10 - 4......and goodbye!"

THINKING OF A RENDEZVOUS

Words and Music by SONNY THROCKMORTON
and BOBBY BRADDOCK

Moderately

1. I ___ said, "Hel - lo, my it's been such a long time." ___
2. (You_ said,) "Are you still ___ work - ing down at the fac - to - ry?"
3. (And you said,) "Got- ta go ___ sure been nice ___ to see you; ___

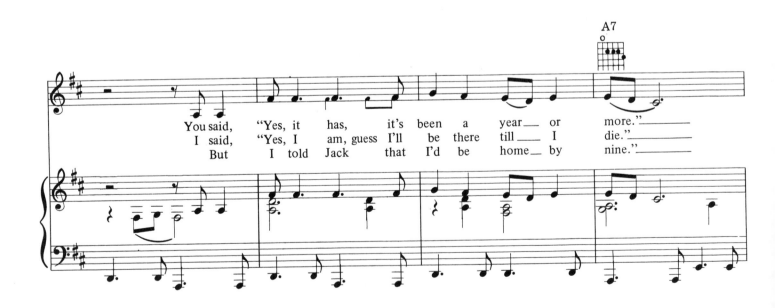

You said, "Yes, it has, it's been a year ___ or more." ___
I said, "Yes, I am, guess I'll be there till ___ I die." ___
But I told Jack that I'd be home by nine." ___

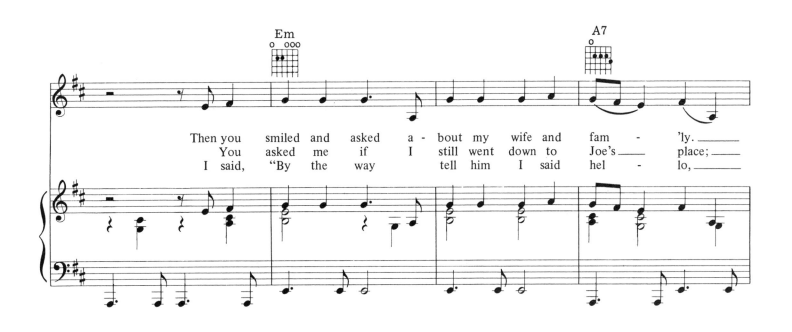

Then you smiled and asked a-bout my wife and fam-'ly.
You asked me if I still went down to Joe's place;
I said, "By the way tell him I said hel-lo,

I said, "John-ny's six and Ju-dy's al-most four."
I said, "Yeah, I do, but it's been a long, long time."
And we'll all have to get to-geth-er some-time."

Chorus

But I was think-ing how I'd love to get you a-lone for one hour,

TILL I GET IT RIGHT

Words and Music by RED LANE
and LARRY HENLEY

Very Slow and Legato

1. I'll just keep on _____ fall-in' in love
2. My door to love _____ has o-pened out

till I get it right. _____
more times than in. _____

Right now I'm like
I'm ei-ther fool

a wound-ed bird hun-gry for the sky. _____
or wise e-nough to o-pen it a-gain, _____

But if I
'Cause _____ I'll

TULSA TIME

Words and Music by
DANNY FLOWERS

WHEN THE TINGLE BECOMES A CHILL

Words and Music by
LOLA JEAN DILLON

WHAT A DIFFERENCE YOU'VE MADE IN MY LIFE

Words and Music by
ARCHIE JORDAN

YOU NEVER MISS A REAL GOOD THING

(TILL HE SAYS GOODBYE)

Words and Music by
BOB McDILL

YOU'RE MY BEST FRIEND

Words and Music by
WAYLAND HOLYFIELD